PAIRED PASSAGES

Grade 2

D1406763

Credits
Content Editor: Hope Spencer
Copy Editor: Jasmine Suarez, Julie B. Killian

Visit *carsondellosa.com* for correlations to Common Core, state, national, and Canadian provincial standards.

Carson-Dellosa Publishing, LLC
PO Box 35665
Greensboro, NC 27425 USA
carsondellosa.com

Printed in the USA • All rights reserved.   ISBN 978-1-4838-3066-7
                                                             01-067161151

Table of Contents

Introduction

As students sharpen their reading comprehension skills, they become better readers. Improving these skills has never been more important as teachers struggle to meet the rigorous college- and career-ready expectations of today's educational standards.

This book offers pairings of high-interest fiction and nonfiction passages that will appeal to even the most reluctant readers. The passages have grade-level readability. Follow-up pages promote specific questioning based on evidence from the passages.

Throughout the book, students are encouraged to practice close reading, focusing on details to make inferences from each passage separately and then as a set. The text-dependent questions and activities that follow the passages encourage students to synthesize the information they have read, leading to deeper comprehension.

How to Use This Book

Three types of pairings divide this book: fiction with nonfiction, nonfiction with nonfiction, and fiction with fiction. The book is broken down further into 22 sets of paired passages that are combined with follow-up questions and activities. Each reading passage is labeled Fiction or Nonfiction.

The passages in this book may be used in any order but should be completed as four-page sets so that students read the passages in the correct pairs. The pairs of passages have been carefully chosen and each pair has topics or elements in common.

Two pages of questions and activities follow each pair of passages to support student comprehension. The questions and activities are based on evidence that students can find in the texts. No further research is required. Students will answer a set of questions that enable comprehension of each of the two passages. The questions range in format and include true/false, multiple choice, and short answer. The final questions or activities ask students to compare and contrast details or elements from the two passages.

Assessment Rubric

Use this rubric as a guide for assessing students' work. It can also be offered to students to help them check their work or as a tool to show your scoring.

4	_____	Independently reads and comprehends grade-level texts
	_____	Easily compares and contrasts authors' purposes
	_____	Uses higher-order thinking skills to link common themes or ideas
	_____	References both passages when comparing and contrasting
	_____	Skillfully summarizes reading based on textual evidence
3	_____	Needs little support for comprehension of grade-level texts
	_____	Notes some comparisons of authors' purposes
	_____	Infers broad common themes or ideas
	_____	Connects key ideas and general themes of both passages
	_____	Uses textual evidence to summarize reading with some support
2	_____	Needs some support for comprehension of grade-level texts
	_____	Understands overt similarities in authors' purposes
	_____	Links stated or obvious common themes or ideas
	_____	Compares and contrasts both passages with support
	_____	Summarizes reading based on textual evidence with difficulty
1	_____	Reads and comprehends grade-level text with assistance
	_____	Cannot compare or contrast authors' purposes
	_____	Has difficulty linking common themes or ideas
	_____	Cannot connect the information from both passages
	_____	Is unable to use textual evidence to summarize reading

Waiting on the Nest

The female snowy owl shivers against the wind. She peeks into the nest beneath her. She does not look for long because she knows the eggs need to stay warm. She hears a sound and looks up. The male owl is flying back to the nest.

"Look what I've caught for you," he says. The male owl drops a shining, silver fish on the ground near the nest.

"Oh, thank you," she says happily. "I am very hungry." The female owl begins to eat the fish. Suddenly, she stops.

"Oh my," she says, "the eggs are hatching!"

She moves over. The owls watch as the eggs slowly hatch. Three owlets are in the nest, each covered with soft white down.

The new parents know they have work to do. They must teach the babies to care for themselves. They will also teach them to fly. For now, the parents enjoy being proud of their new babies.

Snowy Owl Babies

A female snowy owl lays three to 11 eggs. She is more likely to lay eggs when there is a good food supply. Snowy owls eat lemmings. They also eat rabbits, birds, and fish. A female will not lay eggs if there is no food. She lays the eggs in a nest. The nest is on the ground.

The female owl sits on the nest. She will sit on the nest until the eggs hatch. She keeps the eggs safe and warm. The male owl brings food to the female. The female sits on the nest for about a month. Then, the eggs hatch.

The baby owls are soft and white. They are covered in down instead of feathers. Soon, the babies grow feathers. Then, they are light brown.

The babies leave the nest in about a month. They can fly well when they are six weeks old. The parents care for the babies until they are 10 weeks old.

Name _____

Write *true* or *false*.

1. _____ Snowy owls usually have one baby at a time.

2. _____ Snowy owls eat rabbits, fish, and lemmings.

3. _____ The mother snowy owl sits on the nest until the babies are born.

4. _____ The new baby owls have light brown feathers.

Answer each question.

5. Look back at "Snowy Owl Babies." Why would a mother owl wait to have babies?

   A. She would wait to find a good nest.
   B. She would wait until there was a good food supply.
   C. She would wait until the father owl brought her a fish.
   D. She would wait to find another mother owl that would help her.

6. Look back at "Waiting on the Nest." How does the mother owl get food when she is sitting on the nest?

   A. The father owl brings a fish to her.
   B. She eats some of the grass around the nest.
   C. She eats a lemming.
   D. Other owls bring food to the nest.

7. Look back at both passages. Who takes care of the eggs until they hatch?

   A. both parents
   B. the father snowy owl
   C. the mother snowy owl
   D. neither of the parents

8. Look back at both passages. In each egg, write one fact that you learned about snowy owl babies.

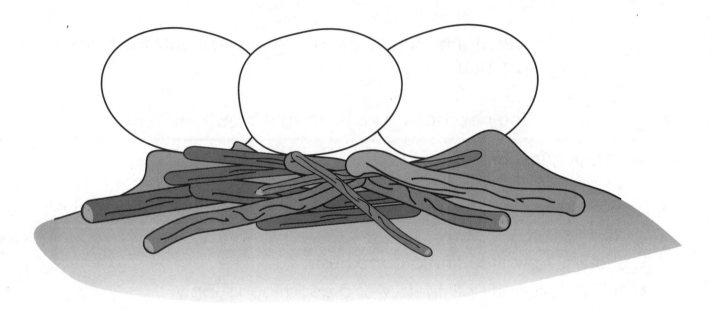

9. Write about snowy owl babies. Use the information you learned in both passages to help you.

_____

_____

_____

_____

My Colorful Friend

On summer days,
I watch the sky,
I know that a ladybug
will soon fly by.

Her red and black wings
flap by my hand.
And she looks for a leaf,
where she can land.

She crawls onto
a leaf in a tree.
I watch her as far
as my eye can see.

As she moves,
I count her spots.
This ladybug
has got a lot!

When I draw ladybugs
at home or school,
they're never like these,
but they're always cool!

The bugs I draw
are green and blue.
Some have big spots,
and some have stripes too!

I love the bugs
I paint and draw,
but I have to admit,
they have one flaw.

As pretty as my
ladybugs are,
they stay on my pad,
and they can never fly far.

So, when the summer sun
warms the sky
I sit on the grass
and wait for my —
lovely flying friend.

Guarding a Bug's Life

An insect's life can be hard. Some animals try to eat insects. Birds and bats are some of their hunters. People may stomp on insects. Some people spray them with bug spray.

Insects have ways of guarding themselves. Some can give off a bad smell. Stinkbugs can give off a foul odor. This odor may keep their hunters from eating the bugs.

Termites and roaches have other ways to protect themselves. These insects can produce a spray. The spray bothers their hunters. Stick insects and beetles can produce this spray too.

Some insects are colorful. They use their colors to protect themselves. Ladybugs are bright red and black. Monarch butterflies are bright orange and black. These colors warn others not to eat them. These insects are poisonous to their hunters.

Other insects can cause pain. Bees and wasps can sting. Some ants can sting too. Their venom can burn or itch. Sometimes, their venom can trigger reactions in their victims.

Many creatures try to eat or harm insects. Insects must have ways to guard themselves.

Name _____

Answer each question.

1. Why do you think the author wrote "My Colorful Friend"?

   A. to entertain the reader with a fun poem about ladybugs

   B. to inform the reader about a ladybug's life cycle

   C. to explain a ladybug's colors to the reader

   D. to inform the reader about summer insects

2. Why do you think the author wrote "Guarding a Bug's Life"?

   A. to entertain the reader with stories about different types of bugs

   B. to inform the reader about different bugs and the way they protect themselves

   C. to explain to the reader that ladybugs and monarch butterflies are not the same color

   D. to entertain readers who like bugs

3. What is the main idea of "Guarding a Bug's Life"?

   A. Some insects give off a foul odor.

   B. Ladybugs and monarch butterflies are poisonous.

   C. Insects have different ways of guarding against predators.

   D. Some insects are red and orange.

4. Copy the main idea from question 3. Then, write two details that support the main idea.

   Main idea: _____

   _____

   Detail: _____

   _____

   Detail: _____

   _____

Name _____

5. Look back at both passages. How are they alike? How are they different? Complete the graphic organizer.

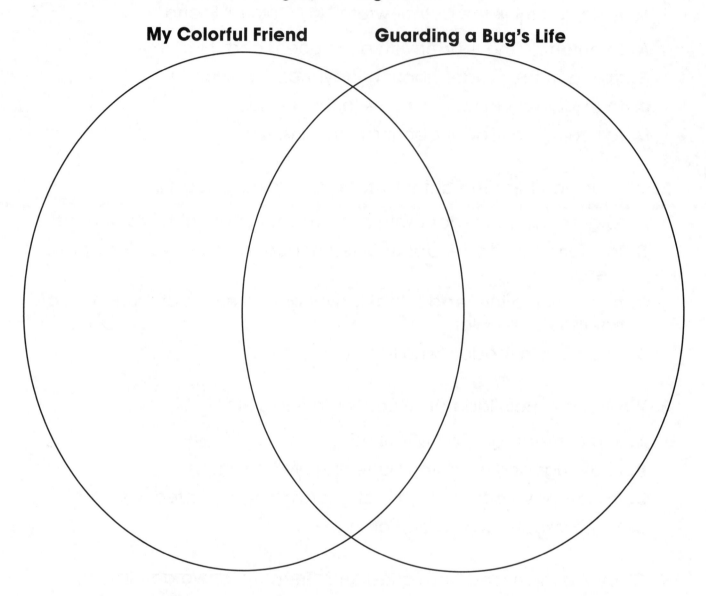

My Colorful Friend   **Guarding a Bug's Life**

6. Which passage would you tell your friend to read? Write a note to tell your friend why you liked one passage more than the other.

_____

_____

_____

_____

_____

Boom!

Boom!

James jumped out of bed and peered out the window. The rain pelted the glass, and a flash of lightning lit up the sky.

James turned around when his door opened. His little sister stood in the doorway. "James," she said, "I hear thunder."

"It's OK," he said. "Come on." James took his sister's hand and led her back to her room. Then, he tucked her into bed.

James sat on the edge of his sister's bed. Suddenly, a loud clap of thunder shook the house. Grace jumped, and her eyes widened. She grabbed James's hand.

"Remember, thunder is a vibration," James said. "It is air that's moving. Tell me some storm safety rules."

Grace recited, "Stay away from water. Stay in a sturdy building or in a car that has closed windows. Stay away from metal. Don't use a phone that has a cord."

"That's good," James said. "Listen, the rain stopped. We can go to sleep now."

James stood up to walk back to his room. He smiled when he realized that Grace was already snoring.

Raining and Pouring

Thunderstorms can happen any time. Storms are more likely to happen in the spring or summer. They are also more likely to happen later in the day.

Three things make a storm. First, the air needs to be moist. Moist air helps clouds and rain form. Then, the air needs to be warm. Warm, unstable air rises quickly. The last part is lift. Lift is what makes an airplane move upward. Lift happens when two different air masses meet. Lift can also be made by sea breezes or mountains.

Thunderstorms make lightning. Lightning is a giant spark of electricity. It looks like a fiery bolt in the sky. It starts in a storm cloud. The charge from the cloud reaches down. A charge from the ground reaches up. The charges meet. Lightning strikes.

Lightning causes thunder. The electricity heats the air and makes it suddenly grow bigger. This makes the sound known as thunder.

About 2,000 thunderstorms happen somewhere on Earth each minute. That is a lot of thunderstorms! One in 10 storms are severe storms. The storms bring lightning and thunder.

Name _____

Answer each question.

1. What wakes up James?

    A. his little sister

    B. a clap of thunder

    C. a door slamming shut

    D. a bird singing

2. Why do you think Grace goes to James's room?

    A. She wants to tell him that she hears thunder.

    B. She is scared, and he is her big brother.

    C. She hears him get up.

    D. She is worried about him.

3. Thunderstorms are more likely to happen

    A. in the spring.

    B. in the winter.

    C. late in the week.

    D. in December.

4. What is lightning?

    A. an electric current

    B. moving air

    C. frozen raindrops

    D. a ball of fire

Write *true* or *false*.

5. _____ About 2,000 thunderstorms happen every year.

6. _____ Lightning causes thunder.

7. Look back at both passages. Complete the graphic organizer with information you learned about storms.

Boom!	Raining and Pouring

8. Look back at "Boom!" Imagine that you are helping James explain the storm to Grace. Use the information in "Raining and Pouring" to help you write sentences about what you could tell Grace when she is scared.

_____

_____

_____

_____

_____

_____

_____

_____

The Smartest Choice

Rachel walks into a store. She looks at the hole in her shoes. She is there to buy new shoes. She cannot attend soccer practice tonight with the shoes she is wearing.

Suddenly, Rachel sees a new game. She loves to play games! Rachel hopes that she has enough money to buy shoes and the game.

Rachel rides the escalator to the shoe department. The soccer shoes are in the front of the shoe area. Rachel sees the shoes that the coach has told the team to wear. She looks at the price, but she is disappointed. If she buys these shoes, she cannot buy the game.

Next to the shoes, she sees another pair. They are not as nice as the first shoes. Rachel can tell that they will not last very long. They may not even last through the soccer season. She looks at the price. If she buys these shoes, she can buy the game too. Rachel is not sure what to do.

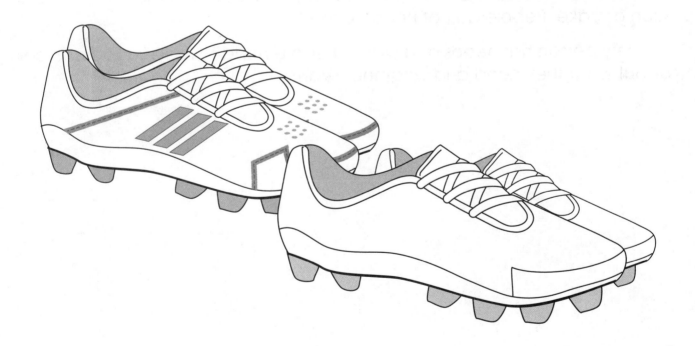

Needs and Wants

Everyone has needs and wants. People spend money to meet their needs. They also spend money to meet their wants. When people have their needs and wants met, they may help their communities.

A need is something a person has to have. For example, people need shelter. They also need water. People need food. Shelter, water, and food are needs.

A want is something a person would like to have. It is not something the person needs to survive. But, it is something the person would enjoy. For example, some people love books. They may even think they cannot live without them. But, books do not help people survive. Books are wants.

Something may be both a need and want. Food is a good example. People need to eat food. Some foods, such as fruits, give people vitamins. People need vitamins. Other foods may be treats. People may want treats such as cake. People do not need cake.

Every person has needs and wants. People need to make good choices about what they need and what they want.

Name _____

Use the word bank to complete the sentences.

| both | needs | shelter | want |

1. People have _____ and wants.

2. People need _____.

3. A _____ is something a person would like to have.

4. A thing such as food could be _____ a need and a want.

Answer each question.

5. Look back at both passages. Are Rachel's new shoes a want or a need? Explain your answer.

_____

_____

_____

6. Is the game a want or a need? Explain your answer.

_____

_____

_____

Name _____

7. In each box, write one item from either passage that could be a need or a want. Then, explain why the item is a need or a want.

Needs	Wants
Item _____ _____ _____	Item _____ _____ _____
Item _____ _____ _____	Item _____ _____ _____
Item _____ _____ _____	Item _____ _____ _____

8. Look back at "The Smartest Choice." What do you think Rachel should buy? Use the information you learned in "Needs and Wants" to help you explain your answer.

_____

_____

_____

_____

_____

_____

The Town Mouse and the Country Mouse
by Aesop (adapted)

Once lived a town mouse. He had a cousin that was a country mouse. The town mouse went to visit his cousin.

"I wish I could have a great feast for you, Cousin," said the country mouse. "We must wait for the harvest before we can eat."

The country mouse showed his cousin his home. The town mouse saw bare fields and empty cupboards. He said, "Cousin! You must come to town for a visit! I eat like a king!"

The country mouse planned to visit his cousin at once! When he arrived, the town mouse filled every tabletop with cheese, fruit, and bread. The country mouse felt his nose begin to twitch as he watched. Suddenly, he heard a noise behind the doorway!

"It's the cat!" yelled the town mouse. "Run!" The town mouse led the way to a small hole in the wall, and the cousins rushed through it.

The country mouse shook with terror. "I'm sorry," he said. "I am going home. Too much danger is here for me to enjoy the feast!"

All Kinds of Communities

A community is a place where people live, work, or have fun together. People live in different kinds of communities. Some people live in a city. Some people live in the country. The two areas are very different from each other.

A city is a busy place. People may live in apartments. They may live in houses. A city has a lot of stores and offices. Some people are lawyers. Others may be doctors, chefs, or store owners. People travel in cars, buses, and trains.

Many things happen in the country. People may live in houses. They may live on farms. The country has some stores and offices. Some people are farmers. Others may be animal doctors, teachers, or store owners. People travel in cars, tractors, and wagons.

Where you live makes a difference in how you live. Think about the community you live in. Do you live in the city or in the country? Whatever your answer, it is probably a good place to live.

Answer each question.

1. Look back at "The Town Mouse and the Country Mouse." What do you think the country mouse means when he says, "We must wait for the harvest before we can eat"?

_____

_____

_____

2. Look back at "The Town Mouse and the Country Mouse." What lesson do you think the author is trying to teach?

_____

_____

_____

3. Do you live in the country or the city? Describe what it is like.

_____

_____

_____

_____

4. Look back at "All Kinds of Communities." Which one has the most people? Explain your answer.

_____

_____

_____

Name _____

5. Look back at both passages. Complete the graphic organizer with descriptions and information.

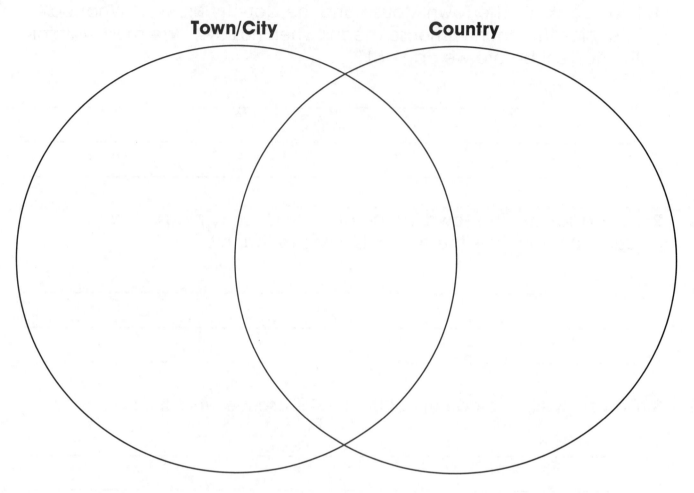

Town/City   **Country**

6. Use the information in the Venn diagram to write about the ways the city and the country are alike.

_____

_____

_____

7. Use the information in the Venn diagram to write about the ways the city and the country are different.

_____

_____

_____

The Princess and the Pea
by Hans Christian Andersen (adapted)

Once, a prince lived in a faraway kingdom. He was a real prince, so he had to marry a real princess.

He left home and began to search. He stopped at many places in the hope of finding a real princess. He did not find one. Sadly, he returned home.

One night, a young woman knocked on the gate. She said that she was a real princess and that she had come to meet the prince.

The queen thought of a test. She took the mattress off of the princess's bed and placed a small pea on the bed. Then, she put 20 mattresses on top of the pea. On top of those, she put 20 feather mattresses. That night, the princess slept on the tall bed.

In the morning, the queen asked the princess how she felt. "I feel terrible," said the princess. "That bed is lumpy. I am bruised all over."

The queen knew that only a real princess could feel the pea through that many mattresses. The prince and princess married. They lived happily ever after.

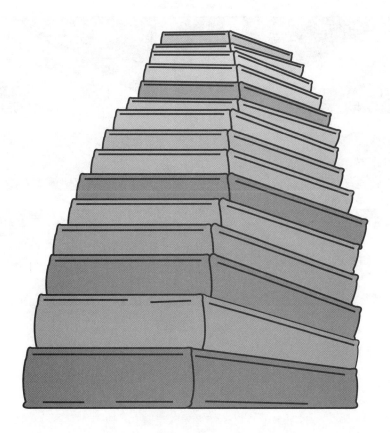

Real Royalty

Prince William is the Prince of Wales. Wales is part of Great Britain. The prince was born in 1982. His father is Prince Charles. His mother was Princess Diana.

The prince went to college in Scotland. At school, he met another student named Catherine. Catherine's friends called her Kate. Catherine and the prince soon became good friends. They spent a lot of time together. They dated for seven years. In 2011, Prince William married Catherine. Now, Catherine is the Duchess of Cambridge.

Prince William had a job. He was in the Royal Air Force. He was a helicopter pilot. Prince William is a hero. In 2011, he was part of a rescue mission. His team rescued two Russian sailors from their sinking boat. In 2012, he helped save a 16-year-old surfer.

The prince is a father. He and Catherine have two children. Prince George was born in 2013. Princess Charlotte was born in 2015.

Name _____

Answer each question.

1. Look back at "The Princess and the Pea." Why do you think the author wrote this passage?

    A. to teach the reader about real princes and princesses

    B. to inform the reader about a test for a real princess

    C. to entertain the reader with a fairy tale about a prince who wanted to marry a real princess

    D. to explain to the reader how a real prince finds a bride

2. Look back at "Real Royalty." Why do you think the author wrote this passage?

    A. to inform the reader about Prince William and his life

    B. to entertain the reader with a story about a prince

    C. to explain to the reader what the job of a prince is

    D. to entertain the reader with a story about a prince who is a father and a hero

3. Look back at "The Princess and the Pea." How did the prince feel after he could not find a real princess? How do you know?

    _____

    _____

4. Look back at "The Princess and the Pea." How do you think the prince felt after he found out that the girl was a real princess? Why?

    _____

    _____

5. Look back at "Real Royalty." Write three words that describe Prince William. Think about the jobs he has had and the things he has done.

    _____   _____   _____

6. Look back at both passages. How are they alike? How are they different? Complete the graphic organizer.

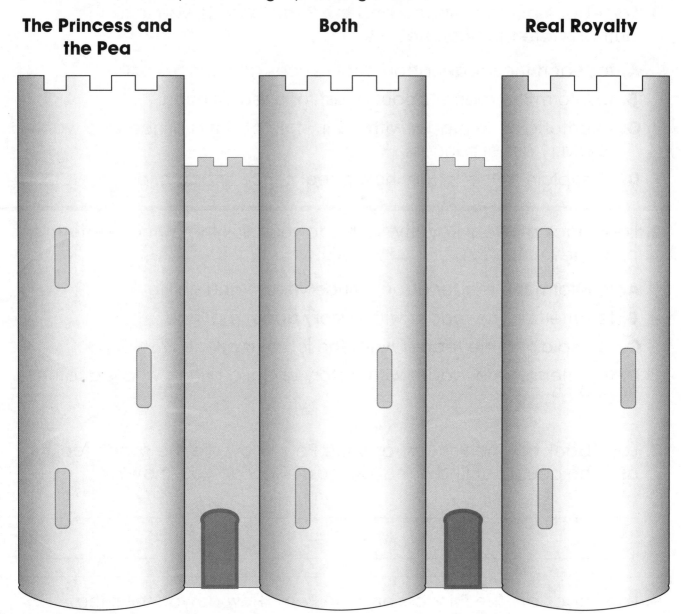

The Princess and the Pea

Both

Real Royalty

7. Look back at both passages. Which one did you enjoy more: the fairy tale or the nonfiction passage? Explain why you enjoyed one more than the other.

_____

_____

_____

_____

Cool in the Pool

When the sun is high,
my friends and I,
follow one rule—
stay cool in the pool!

We never stay dry,
each girl and guy,
sticks with one rule—
stay cool in the pool!

We think it is neat
to beat the heat.
With just one rule—
stay cool in the pool!

We don't have to vote,
we know we will float,
and follow one rule—
stay cool in the pool!

Water tickles our toes
and our happiness grows,
when we follow our rule—
stay cool in the pool!

The heat of summer
is never a bummer.
We know one rule—
stay cool in the pool!

Our green skin is wet,
but we will not fret!
We have one rule—
stay cool in the pool!

When it's time for lunch,
a bug we might munch,
then back to our rule—
stay cool in the pool!

And, each of us frogs
loves to jump on a log
when we follow our rule
and stay cool in our pool!

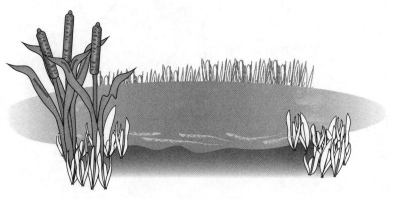

Swimming Safety

Many children love to swim and have fun in the water. But, they must follow water safety rules. Talk to the adults and friends who swim with you. Make sure that everyone knows about safety.

Adults have many jobs. An adult should watch children while they swim. The adult should tell children to stay away from drains. The adult should keep a phone near the pool. Finally, the adult should review basic swimming safety tips with each child.

Adults should learn to swim. They should be sure their children can swim too. Adults should learn skills that could help them save someone. They might take classes to learn CPR. CPR is a way to help someone start breathing again.

Do you have a pool at your house? Talk to your parents to make sure it is safe. Your pool should have a fence around it. You might want to place an alarm in the water. If a child falls into the pool, the alarm would warn an adult.

Swimming is a lot of fun. People must be safe when they swim. Then, everyone can have fun.

Name _____

Answer each question.

1. Look back at "Swimming Safety." What is the main idea of the passage?

    A. Adults have many jobs when children are swimming.

    B. Adults should learn to swim.

    C. Everyone should know about swimming safety rules.

    D. Adults should review basic swimming safety rules with children.

2. Look back at "Swimming Safety." What is *CPR*?

    A. a swimming stroke that helps adults save other swimmers

    B. an alarm that an adult should put in a swimming pool

    C. a way to help a person start breathing again

    D. a swimsuit for a child

3. Look back at "Cool in the Pool." At the beginning of the poem, who did you think the speaker was? Why? _____

    _____

    _____

4. At the end of the poem, who did you think the speaker was? Why?

    _____

    _____

    _____

Write *true* or *false*.

5. _____ An adult should keep a phone nearby when watching swimmers.

6. _____ When children are swimming, adults should check on them every 10 minutes.

7. Look back at both passages. Think about the swimming rules you learned. Complete the graphic organizer.

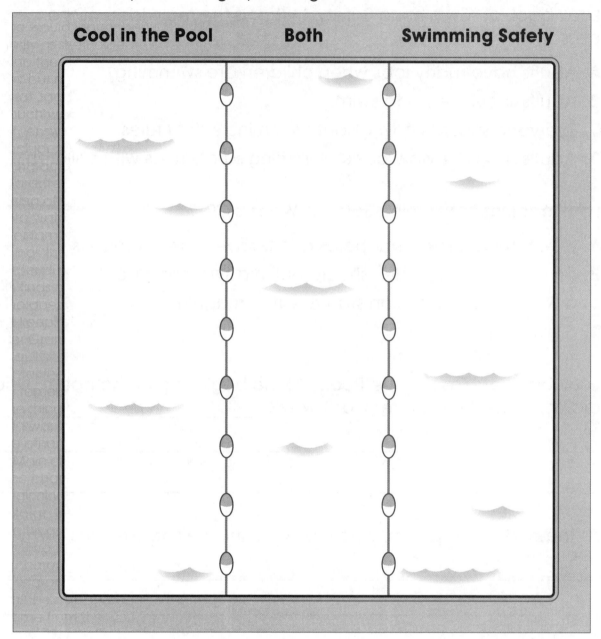

Cool in the Pool	Both	Swimming Safety

8. What do you think is the most important swimming rule of all? Explain your answer.

_____

_____

_____

_____

Riding My Bicycle

I don't want to swim, read, or hike;

I just want to ride my bike!

But, Mom says there is a lot to know

before I can get on and go.

She says, "Bring a helmet that fits just right.

Make sure your bike is the perfect height.

Check your tires—they may need air,

oil the chain and check it with care.

Ask your folks just where you should ride,

they'll help you choose a safe place outside."

"Watch the road in front of you,

so every obstacle is in full view.

Keep both hands on the handlebars,

stop and check both ways for cars.

Obey traffic signs and stop at red lights,

when you ride on the street, ride on the right.

Use bike routes or bike lanes when you can,

and when you turn, signal with your hand!

Riding your bike can be lots of fun,

but being safe is best for everyone!"

Bicycle Safety

It is important to be safe when you ride your bicycle. You need to wear a helmet. A helmet protects your head. Your head protects your brain! Wear a helmet that fits you properly and keep the straps fastened.

Choose a bike that is the right size for you. Stand with one foot on either side of the bike. You should have about one to three inches between you and the top bar.

Ask an adult to help you take care of your bike. Make sure that each part of your bike is tightly attached. Check the chain and oil it regularly. Ask an adult to help you check your brakes. Make sure that they are not sticking. Then, check the air pressure in the tires.

When you ride, be sure to wear bright colors. Be careful that shoelaces, pant legs, and straps cannot be caught in the chain.

Before you ride, learn bike safety rules and hand signals. Then, gather some friends and hit the road!

Name _____

Use the word bank to complete the sentences.

adult	bright	helmet

1. A _____ protects your head.

2. Ask an _____ to help you take care of your bike.

3. When you ride, wear _____ colors.

Circle the letter of the line that rhymes with the first line.

4. She says, "Bring a helmet that fits just right."

    A. before I can get on and go.
    B. Make sure your bike is the perfect height.
    C. Check your tires—they may need air,
    D. oil the chain and check it with care.

5. Watch the road in front of you,

    A. so every obstacle is in full view.
    B. Keep both hands on the handlebars.
    C. they'll help you choose a safe place outside.
    D. stop and check both ways for cars.

6. Riding your bike can be lots of fun,

    A. and when you turn, signal with your hand!
    B. but being safe is best for everyone!
    C. use bike routes or bike lanes when you can,
    D. when you ride on the street, ride on the right.

Name _____

7. Look back at both passages. Complete the graphic organizer.

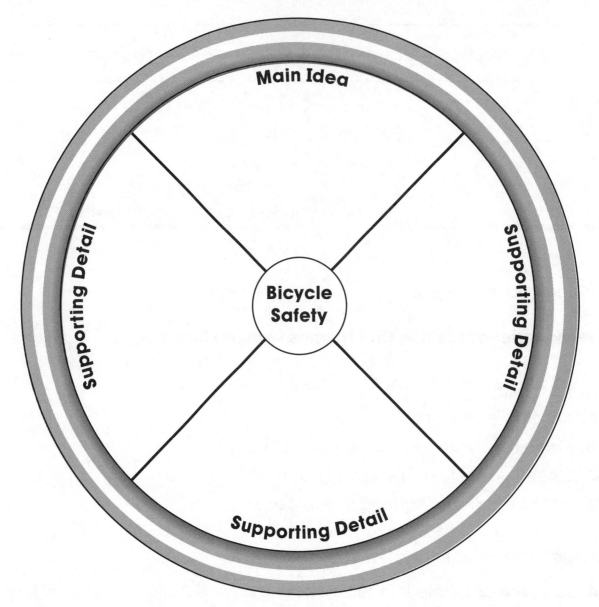

8. Imagine that you have been asked to teach a younger friend about bicycle safety. Think about both passages. Write a short note to your friend.

_____

_____

_____

_____

_____

A Patriotic Celebration

The Fourth of July is a fun and important US holiday. It honors the day that America declared its independence from Great Britain. In 1870, the day was declared a legal holiday. It is also known as Independence Day.

The first celebration happened in 1776. Colonel John Nixon read the Declaration of Independence aloud. People rang bells and bands played.

Today, some towns hold parades. Marching bands play music, and people make speeches. Some people hang flags on their homes. They put flags in their yards too. People wear red, white, and blue. Many people have cookouts to celebrate. They may have picnics. Some people play baseball. Because it is summer, many people are outside.

At night, people may have fireworks. Some people use firecrackers. Others use sparklers. Some people like to watch fireworks in the sky.

Washington, DC has a grand fireworks display every year. New York City does too. Other cities have smaller displays as well. A lot of people gather in parks and fields to watch fireworks. Others may watch displays on TV.

Light Up the Night!

Fireworks come in many types. One type makes a loud noise. A second type makes sparks. A third type makes a show in the night sky.

Firecrackers make loud bangs. They have been around for a long time. A firecracker has flash powder. The powder is inside a paper tube, and a fuse is on the end.

Sparklers burn slowly. They may burn for a minute. A sparkler is made on a metal wire. The wire gets hot when the sparkler burns. The hot wire could burn someone. It is a good idea to throw the used wire into a bucket of water.

Fireworks in the sky are called aerial fireworks. Basic fireworks have shells that are launched from mortars. People mix powders in the shells to make colors. Orange is the easiest color to make. Purple and blue are the hardest to make. But, you will see all colors!

Name _____

Use the word bank to complete the sentences.

| aerial | flags | Independence Day | sparklers |

I. The Fourth of July is also called _____.

2. People put _____ in their yards on the Fourth of July.

3. _____ burn slowly.

4. Fireworks in the sky are called _____ fireworks.

Answer each question.

5. Look back at "A Patriotic Celebration." Write three ways people celebrate the Fourth of July.

_____

_____

_____

6. Why do you think the author wrote "A Patriotic Celebration"? Explain your answer.

_____

_____

7. Why do you think the author wrote "Light Up the Night!"? Explain your answer.

_____

_____

8. Look back at both passages. In the graphic organizer, write words and phrases that describe each type of firework.

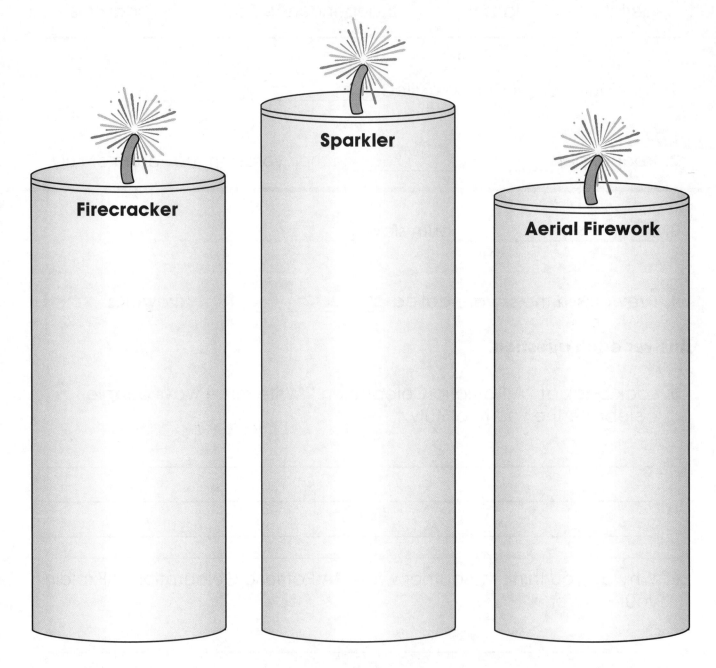

Firecracker

Sparkler

Aerial Firework

9. Look at your answers to questions 6 and 7. Explain how the authors' purposes are alike or different.

_____

_____

_____

A Pet to Bark About

There are many types of dogs. There are more than 300 breeds! Caring for a dog is a big job. Dogs depend on people to keep them healthy and happy.

If you have a dog, you must take him or her to the vet at least once a year. A vet is an animal doctor. The vet will give your dog a shot that will keep her from getting sick. The vet will check your dog's teeth. You must give your dog medicine once a month. The medicine will keep your dog from getting fleas. It will also keep your dog from getting worms in her tummy.

Every day, you should give your dog food and fresh water. You should play with your dog and give her lots of exercise. You should also bathe and brush your dog.

Dogs cannot talk, but they do bark, growl, and whine. They also communicate with their ears, faces, and tails. You can train a dog to do tricks and to obey. You must train your dog to go to the bathroom outside of the house.

Caring for a dog is a big responsibility! But, it is very rewarding.

A Pet to Purr About

Cats were first tamed in Egypt. Since then, people have kept cats as pets. There are many types of cats. Caring for a pet cat is a big job! Cats need people to keep them happy and healthy.

If you have a cat, you must take him or her to the vet once each year. The vet is an animal doctor. The vet will give your cat a shot that will help keep him healthy. The vet will look at your cat's teeth. Your cat will need to take medicine once each month. The medicine will keep him from getting fleas. It will also keep him from getting worms in his heart.

Your cat will need good food and fresh water. Cats bathe themselves, but you may need to brush your cat's fur. Indoor cats go to the bathroom inside a litter box. You should make sure that your cat always has a clean litter box.

A cat will communicate with you by meowing and purring. A cat also uses his body to tell you if he is happy, scared, or angry.

You have many things to remember when you live with a cat. But, a cat is also a lot of fun!

Name _____

Use the word bank to complete the sentences.

| animal | bathe | communicate | medicine | vet |

1. A vet is an _____ doctor.

2. You must give dogs _____ that will keep them from getting fleas.

3. Dogs _____ with their ears, faces, and tails.

4. You must take your cat to the _____ once each year.

5. Cats _____ themselves, but you may need to brush them.

Write true or false.

6. _____ A vet is an animal doctor.

7. _____ There are over 300 dog breeds.

8. _____ Cats were first tamed in Japan.

9. Look back at both passages. How are they alike? How are they different? Complete the Venn diagram.

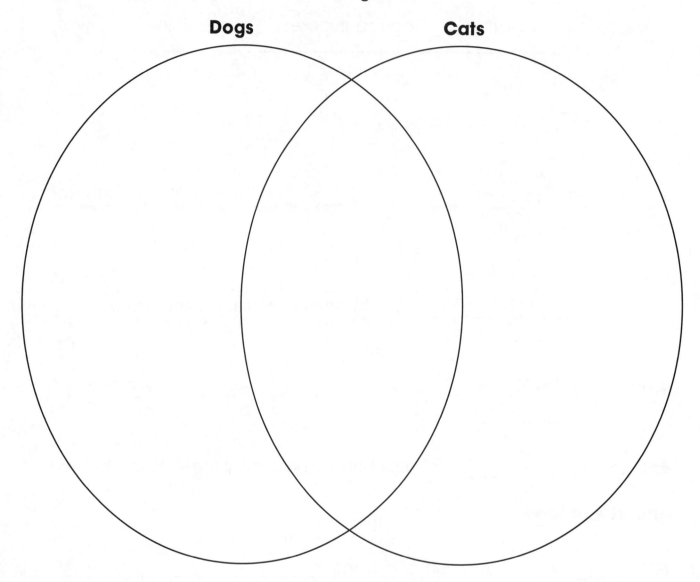

Dogs   **Cats**

10. Imagine that you can have a pet dog or a pet cat. Which one would you choose? Explain why you chose one instead of the other. Use evidence from both passages and the Venn diagram.

_____

_____

_____

_____

From Tadpole to Frog

Frogs are amphibians. Most amphibians start life in the water and have tails and gills. Later, amphibians grow lungs and legs, and they can live on land. Frogs lay their eggs in the water. The female frog lays thousands of eggs. The eggs hatch in about 10 days.

Each egg hatches into a tadpole. Tadpoles have gills and long tails. They do not look like adult frogs yet. They do look more like fish. The tadpole uses its tail to swim. Over time, the tadpole's tail begins to shrink.

As the tadpole grows, its back legs begin to grow. The tadpole becomes a froglet. Lungs begin to develop, and front legs grow. The froglet's eyes and mouth become larger. Its tail keeps shrinking.

When the tail is gone, the froglet becomes a frog. The adult frog can leap out of the water. It can live on land, but it must live near water so that it can keep its skin moist. Adult frogs live near ponds and swamps.

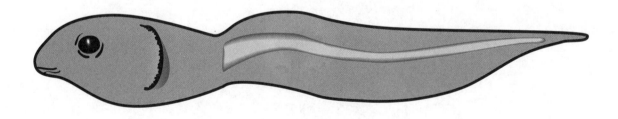

From Egg to Butterfly

A butterfly's life cycle has four stages. The first stage is the egg. The female butterfly lays her egg on a leaf or stem. The egg is tiny and round or shaped like an oval. It is either smooth or has a ribbed texture.

The second stage of a butterfly's life cycle is the larva. It is also called the caterpillar. A caterpillar hatches from the egg. The caterpillar is tiny. It eats a lot of leaves and grass where it hatched. Then, the caterpillar grows. It sheds its skin three or four times as it gets bigger.

The caterpillar stops growing. It forms itself into a chrysalis. This third stage is the pupa. The caterpillar's wings grow. Its lungs and organs change. These changes are called metamorphosis.

A butterfly hatches during the last stage of the life cycle. When the butterfly comes out of the chrysalis, its wings are soft. It pumps blood into its wings. In three or four hours, the wings are firm. Then, the butterfly is ready to fly!

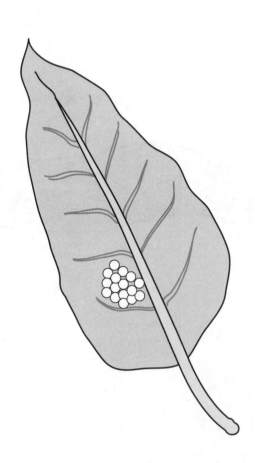

Name _____

Answer each question.

1. Most amphibians start life in the _____ and then can live on land and in water.

    A. egg

    B. shell

    C. water

    D. pupa

2. A frog's egg hatches into a

    A. tadpole.

    B. froglet.

    C. pupa.

    D. larva.

3. Look back at "From Tadpole to Frog." Why do you think the author wrote this passage?

    A. to entertain the reader with stories about pond animals

    B. to explain to the reader how life cycles occur

    C. to inform the reader about the stages of a frog's life cycle

    D. none of the above

4. Why do you think the female butterfly lays its eggs on a leaf or stem?

    A. so that it can reach the leaves and stems

    B. because it knows that the caterpillar will need to eat leaves and stems when it hatches from the egg

    C. because it wants to lay its eggs in a pretty place

    D. all of the above

Name _____

5. Look back at both passages. Complete the graphic organizer.

Frog	**Butterfly**
First stage:	First stage:
Second stage:	Second stage:
Third stage:	Third stage:
Fourth stage:	Fourth stage:

6. Write a summary of the information you learned from both passages.

_____

_____

_____

_____

7. What questions do you still have?

_____

_____

Vacuum Cleaner Kid

Kyle Krichbaum loves vacuum cleaners. He has always loved them. He collects them.

He loved vacuum cleaners when he was a baby. He received his first vacuum cleaner as a gift when he was just a baby. The vacuum cleaner was a toy. He followed his mom when she turned on the real one. He dressed as a vacuum cleaner for a costume party.

When he was six, he went to school. He did not want to go out for recess. Instead, he wanted to vacuum the classroom! He even vacuumed the principal's office.

Now, Kyle collects vacuum cleaners. Kyle is paid to fix vacuum cleaners too. He uses the money to buy more vacuum cleaners. His collection is one of the largest in the world! The collection is worth a lot of money. His best vacuum cleaner is worth about $10,000!

Kyle is the youngest person who collects vacuum cleaners. He keeps them all over his house. He even keeps some at his grandmother's house. He uses some of them when he cleans.

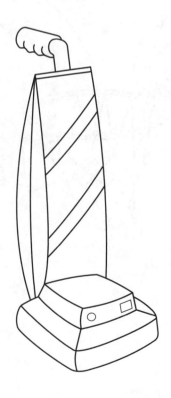

Dribbling Down the Court

Julian Newman loves basketball. When Julian was three, his father knew that Julian might be a good player. His father painted court lines in the front yard. Julian plays every day. He does not stop when he goes to his room before bed. In his room, he tosses a foam ball at the ceiling. Then, he goes to sleep.

His mom and dad were both good basketball players. They met on the basketball court. His dad is a teacher. He coaches the varsity team at Julian's school.

When Julian was 11, he played for his middle school team. Julian played very well. Coaches then moved him to the varsity team at a nearby private high school! He was the shortest player on the team. Soon, he was starting for the team. The team had a winning season!

Julian has appeared on a TV talk show. He has also performed during an NBA basketball game. No one knows for sure what to expect from Julian. People are sure to be watching him!

Name _____

Read each pair of events. Underline the event that happened first.

1. Kyle went to school.

Kyle received a toy vacuum cleaner as a gift.

2. Kyle fixes other people's vacuum cleaners.

Kyle followed his mom when she turned the real vacuum cleaner on.

3. Coaches moved Julian to the varsity team.

Julian's father thought Julian might be a good player.

4. Julian's team had a winning season.

His father painted court lines in the front yard.

Answer each question.

5. Look back at "Vacuum Cleaner Kid." What is the main idea of the passage?

　A. Kyle has a collection of vacuum cleaners.

　B. Kyle loves vacuum cleaners.

　C. Kyle has a vacuum cleaner that is worth a lot of money.

　D. Kyle wanted to vacuum the classroom instead of go outside for recess.

6. Look back at "Dribbling Down the Court." What is the main idea of the passage?

　A. Julian loves basketball.

　B. Julian plays basketball every day.

　C. Julian plays on a varsity basketball team.

　D. Julian has basketball lines painted in his front yard.

Name _____

7. Look back at both passages. How are they alike? How are they different? Complete the Venn diagram.

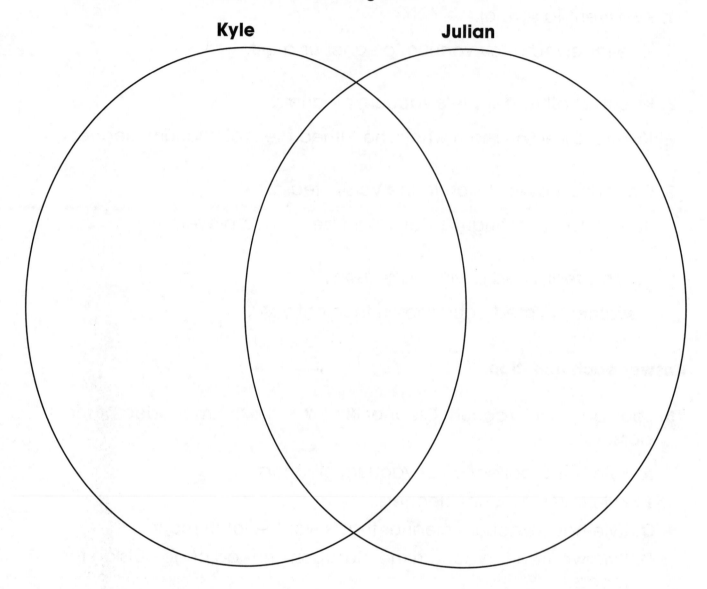

Kyle

Julian

8. After reading both passages, how do you think people choose one special thing to collect or one sport to play?

_____

_____

_____

_____

_____

How Seeds Travel

Each plant, tree, and flower starts as a seed. Not all seeds begin the same way.

People plant some seeds. You may have planted seeds in your yard. Farmers plant seeds in their fields.

Some seeds travel to new places to grow. Seeds may travel by hitching a ride on an animal. A seed may be sticky or spiky. When an animal walks by, the seed sticks to the animal's fur. A sticky seed may also stick to a person's socks or clothing. The seed can travel that way.

Seeds may travel on the wind or in water. Some seeds are light. They float easily on the wind or in water.

When animals eat seeds, they help them travel! If the seed is not digested, the animal may drop it somewhere else. Then, the seed grows where it is dropped.

Many animals help seeds travel when they bury them. An animal plans to come back and eat the seeds, but instead forgets about them. The seeds sprout where they are buried.

Seeds have many ways to get around. Wherever they land, new plants, trees, or flowers grow!

How Plants Grow

There are many different types of plants. Trees, flowers, and grass are all examples of plants. They may look different, but they each have the same basic life cycle.

The first stage of a plant's life cycle is the seed. Seeds do not look alike. They are different sizes. They are different colors. Each seed has a plant inside of it.

As water softens the outside of a seed, it begins to crack. A tiny shoot appears through the crack in the seed.

The shoot grows, and it becomes the stem of the plant. Roots begin to form. They grow down into the soil. Over time, the stem becomes stronger and taller. Leaves and flowers begin to appear too.

As the plant grows, its leaves and flowers grow as well. The flowers begin to form the plant's new seeds. Then, the cycle starts all over again, and a new plant is ready to grow.

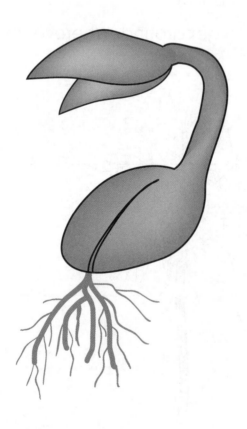

Name _____

Write *true* or *false*.

1. _____ A seed may travel by floating in a puddle.

2. _____ A seed may travel in a person's suitcase.

3. _____ Seeds all look alike.

4. _____ Each plant produces new seeds so that new plants can grow.

5. _____ The stem of a plant produces seeds.

Use the word bank to complete the sentences.

bury	seed	stem

6. Each plant, tree, and flower starts as a _____.

7. Many animals help seeds travel when they _____ them.

8. A shoot grows from the seed and becomes the _____ of the plant.

9. Write two ways seeds travel. Explain your answers.

_____

_____

_____

_____

Name _____

10. Look back at both passages. Think about the information you learned about the way plants grow. Complete the graphic organizer.

How Seeds Travel   How Plants Grow

11. Look back at both passages. Think about the author's purpose for writing each passage. Explain how they are similar or different. Write examples from the passages to support your answer.

_____

_____

_____

_____

An Important Job

The president of the United States has many jobs. He is in charge of all soldiers. He decides where to send them. He makes deals with other countries. These deals are called treaties. The president chooses people to go to other countries. These people speak for the United States. They help everyone understand each other.

The president helps make new laws. First, Congress writes the laws. Then, the president decides whether to sign them. If he signs them, they are laws. He may not sign them. Then, they do not pass.

A group of people helps the president do his job. They are members of his cabinet. The president chooses the people who serve on his cabinet. Then, the Senate must say that his choices are OK.

The president makes many speeches. His speeches tell about his plans for the country. He has many celebrations to attend. He may give awards to special people. The president always has something to do.

Symbols of America

The president of the United States is an American symbol. People think of America when they see the president's picture. Many other symbols belong to America.

The United States flag is called "Old Glory." It has 13 stripes. The stripes stand for the first colonies. The flag has 50 stars. Each star stands for one state. The flag has its own holiday. Flag Day is on June 14.

The bald eagle is the national symbol of the United States of America. The first US lawmakers wanted a national bird. They said that the eagle was a good symbol. It stands for strength, courage, and freedom. The eagle's picture is on the one-dollar bill.

The Statue of Liberty is in New York. It is a symbol of freedom. It stands on an island in the harbor. It was a gift from France. It is made of copper. The statue has 354 stairs inside.

The United States has other symbols as well. The Liberty Bell is a symbol, and the "Star-Spangled Banner" is another symbol. Many monuments are also American symbols.

Name _____

Answer each question.

1. Look back at "An Important Job." Write the main idea of the passage.

   _____

2. Look back at "An Important Job." Write three details that support the main idea.

   A. _____

   _____

   B. _____

   _____

   C. _____

   _____

3. Look back at "Symbols of America." Write the main idea of the passage.

   _____

4. Look back at "Symbols of America." Write three details that support the main idea.

   A. _____

   _____

   B. _____

   _____

   C. _____

   _____

5. Look back at both passages. Complete the graphic organizer.

Topic: Symbols of America
Symbol: Facts about symbol:
Symbol: Facts about symbol:
Symbol: Facts about symbol:
Symbol: Facts about symbol:

6. Imagine that you have been asked to write a short report about American symbols. Use information from both passages to help you write the report.

_____

_____

_____

_____

_____

_____

Desert Habitat

You may think the desert is a very hot place. Many deserts are hot during the day. But, at night, deserts may be very cold. Why?

Deserts are very dry. It may only rain a few times a year in the desert. But, other habitats have more rain. The rain makes the air humid. Humid air traps heat. It can keep the air warm at night. The air in the desert is not humid because very little rain falls.

Animals in the desert have adapted to the extreme heat and searing sun. They can live with little water. Many desert animals are nocturnal. Nocturnal means being active at night. These animals sleep during the day. Other animals live underground.

Many plants grow in the desert. They have adapted to the heat and dry air. Some can collect and store water. Some do not lose water quickly.

Deserts can be hot, cold, and dry. The plants and animals that live there have features that help them thrive.

Wetlands Habitat

Freshwater wetlands are all over the world. They are near rivers, lakes, or streams. Some wetlands change during the year. When a lot of rain falls, the wetlands are underwater. When less rain falls, animals can walk through the wetlands.

Marshes, swamps, and bogs are types of wetlands. Marshes have grassy plants. Swamps have a lot more trees. Bogs are spongy.

Wetlands can keep flooding from happening. They hold water that could cause floods. As water levels fall, wetlands release water.

Wetland plants have adaptations. Some plants grow above the water. But, their roots grow in the soil under the water. Other plants have leaves that float. Other plants grow under the water.

Many wetland animals can live only in water. Others can live in water and on land. Some birds have long legs. These keep them above water when they walk. Others have webbed feet.

Wetlands are everywhere. They may change. The plants and animals that live there have special features. These help them live in the wet, soggy places.

Name _____

Answer each question.

1. Deserts are

   A. hot.

   B. cold.

   C. dry.

   D. all of the above.

2. Nocturnal means

   A. adapted to the desert.

   B. living underground.

   C. sleeping during the day and being active at night.

   D. none of the above.

3. Swamps have more trees than

   A. marshes.

   B. bogs.

   C. marshes and bogs.

   D. none of the above.

4. Wetland plants adapted by

   A. having leaves that float on the water.

   B. having plants that grow above water and roots that grow in the soil.

   C. having plants that grow under the water.

   D. all of the above.

5. Look back at both passages. Complete the graphic organizer.

Deserts	**Wetlands**
Words to know:	Words to know:
Facts I learned:	Facts I learned:
Questions I still have:	Questions I still have:

6. Look at your answers in question 5. Write a summary of what you have learned about these two habitats.

_____

_____

_____

_____

_____

Family Vacation

"Pass the hot dogs, please," Erin said. She pushed her stick through the hot dog and held it over the fire. The hot dog sizzled.

Later, Mom took out the marshmallows. Erin and her sister clapped their hands. Then, Erin, Jan, and Dad each took a marshmallow and roasted it over the fire. Mom passed out graham crackers and chocolate, and Erin squeezed her marshmallow between the graham crackers.

She leaned back and sighed. This was the best time of the year! Erin looked at the stars. She wished she could count them! She listened to the stream.

The stream came from high above them. Erin and Jan could splash and swim in it all morning. Then, they would hike on one of the steep trails with Mom and Dad. Sometimes, they would fish in one of the lakes near their campsite.

Erin knew she would dream about camping fun as she slid into her sleeping bag. Dad zipped up the tent flap, and Mom said, "Good night!" Erin did not answer, though. She was already asleep.

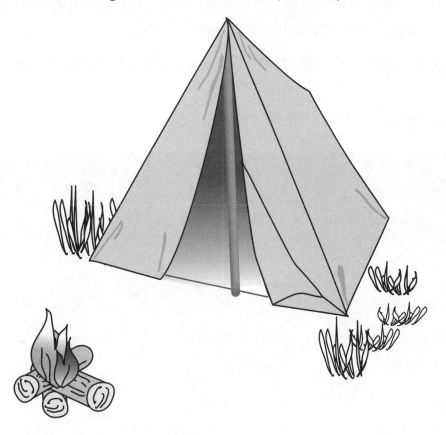

Summer Vacation

Rashad splashed through the waves. He found the ball and threw it back to his brother. Zach jumped and caught it.

"It's time for dinner!" Mother called.

The boys picked up their towels and kicked through the sand. Rashad could smell the hot dogs cooking over the campfire. His stomach grumbled, and he moved more quickly.

"Don't you love summer?" Zach asked.

"Yes, it's the best," Rashad said. "Let's get up early tomorrow. We can collect some seashells before we go fishing."

"That's a great idea!" Zach said.

When they reached their campsite, they each ate two hot dogs. Then, Mom set out a plate of marshmallows, chocolate, and graham crackers. The boys were quiet while they ate their dessert.

Rashad rinsed his swimsuit and brushed his teeth. He helped Zach hang his swimsuit and towel on the clothesline. Then, the brothers slipped into their tent. Each boy crawled into his sleeping bag.

"Sleep well, Zach," Rashad said. "Dream about seashells and crashing waves."

Zach smiled as he drifted off to sleep.

Name _____

Answer each question.

1. In the story, "Family Vacation," where do Erin and her family go on vacation?

   the beach   the big city   the desert   the mountains

   How do you know?

   _____

   _____

   _____

2. In the story, "Summer Vacation," where do Rashad and his family go on vacation?

   the beach   the big city   the desert   the mountains

   How do you know?

   _____

   _____

   _____

3. In the story, "Summer Vacation," which brother do you think is older?

   Rashad   Zach

   How do you know?

   _____

   _____

   _____

Name _____

4. Look back at both passages. Complete the graphic organizer.

Family Vacation	**Summer Vacation**
Beginning	Beginning
Middle	Middle
End	End

5. Write two ways that the passages are alike.

_____

_____

6. Write two ways that the passages are different.

_____

_____

The Hat

"Take off your hat,"
my teacher said.
"We do not wear hats
upon our heads."

"But, teacher," I said,
"this hat is cool.
It helps me think
when I'm at school."

My teacher looked at me
and frowned.
"We do not wear hats,
even if they are crowns!"

"Please, teacher," I said,
and hung my head low,
"this hat is just special,
it simply can't go."

My teacher is good,
and she always is kind,
but I know that she needs
to have students who mind.

She called me right up,
led me out to the hall,
I shook as I stood
with my back to the wall.

"Young man," she said,
"we are in school,
and each boy and girl
must follow the rules."

I pulled off my hat
and waited with dread,
I had a new haircut,
a big mess on my head!

My teacher is kind,
but she's very smart too.
Right away, she saw a cut
that just would not do.

Gently, she replaced my hat,
and then turned to the class to say,
"How could I have forgotten?
Today is class hat day!"

Rapunzel
by the Brothers Grimm (adapted)

Long ago, a couple was about to have a baby. They lived near an old woman. The woman had a lovely garden.

Each day, the wife looked at the garden. She wanted some lettuce. She nagged her husband until he got some. She ate the lettuce and wanted more. Her husband went back to the garden. The old woman caught him. She told him that she would release him if the couple gave her their child.

When the child was born, the old woman took her. She named the child Rapunzel. She locked Rapunzel in a tall tower. Over time, the girl's hair grew. The old woman would climb the girl's hair to get into the tower. When the old woman approached the tower, she called, "Rapunzel, Rapunzel, let down your hair."

A prince watched the old woman. He called, "Rapunzel, Rapunzel, let down your hair." He climbed the tower, and the two fell in love at once. The prince helped Rapunzel escape, and the two lived happily ever after.

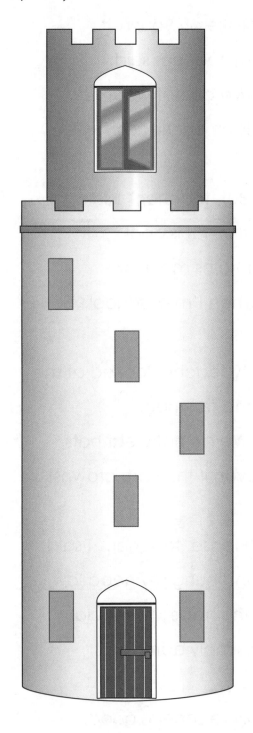

Answer each question.

1. Look back at "The Hat." Why does the teacher want the boy to take his hat off?

   A. It is against the rules to wear a hat in school.

   B. She does not like the hat.

   C. She likes the boy's haircut.

   D. She wants to wear it.

2. Look back at "The Hat." Why does the boy want to wear the hat?

   A. He likes the hat.

   B. He likes to break school rules.

   C. He does not like his teacher.

   D. He does not like his haircut.

3. Look back at "Rapunzel." Why did the couple lose their child?

   A. They did not want her.

   B. The husband was caught in the old woman's garden.

   C. The prince stole her.

   D. The old woman stole her.

4. How did the prince meet Rapunzel?

   A. He saw her in the old woman's garden.

   B. They went to a ball and danced together.

   C. He climbed her hair and went into the tower.

   D. none of the above

Circle the letter of the line that rhymes with the first line.

5. with my back to the wall.

   A. She called me right up,

   B. led me out to the hall,

   C. I shook as I stood

   D. "Young man," she said,

6. but, she's very smart too.

   A. Right away, she saw a cut

   B. My teacher is kind,

   C. that just would not do.

   D. Gently, she replaced my hat,

Name _____

7. Look back at both passages. Complete the graphic organizer.

Title	Main Character	Problem	Solution
The Hat			
Rapunzel			

8. Look back at the graphic organizer. How are the two main characters alike? How are the two main characters different?

_____

_____

_____

_____

_____

_____

Why Fox Wears Red
by Thornton W. Burgess (adapted)

In early times, Mr. Fox's coat was a dull brown. He was polite to the other animals. He never raised his voice. He did not ask rude questions. The other animals hardly noticed him. He listened to them talk. Then, he went to bed early. They all said, "Mr. Fox is such a good neighbor!"

Mr. Fox crept out in the middle of the night. He used the information he heard. He stole the best crops. He ate the best food. The next day, he listened in shock as his neighbors discussed the crimes.

Soon, Mother Nature heard of the crimes. She came to the forest to find out who the culprit was. As she spoke to Miss Chicken about missing eggs, she noticed Mr. Fox. The tip of his tail was covered with red clay. The only red clay in the forest was near Miss Chicken's henhouse. Mother Nature did not want Mr. Fox to go unnoticed anymore. She turned his coat bright red. Since that day, all foxes have been red.

Why Bear Has a Stubby Tail
by Thornton W. Burgess (adapted)

Long ago, Bear was king of the forest. He was happy and only concerned with finding food. He did not worry about not having a tail. He had no need for one! But, one day, he heard Mr. Fox and Mr. Skunk talking.

"What kind of ruler is he?" they laughed. "He doesn't even have a tail!"

Mother Nature saw King Bear sitting sadly. "What is wrong?" she asked.

King Bear knew that he did not need a tail, but he begged Mother Nature to give him one. Mother Nature told him it would be in his way. He begged even more. She finally agreed.

King Bear was proud of his bushy new tail! He showed it to everyone. But, it did get in his way. It also hurt when he sat on it.

He begged Mother Nature to remove it. She finally agreed, but she left a stubby tail behind to remind him of the tail he did not really need. Since then, all bears have had stubby tails.

Name _____

Answer each question.

I. Look back at "Why Fox Wears Red." How do you think Mr. Fox will act the next time he hears people talking? Why? _____

_____

_____

2. Look back at "Why Bear Has a Stubby Tail." How do you think King Bear will act the next time he hears animals making fun of the way he looks? Why? _____

_____

_____

3. Who listened to his neighbors talk?

   A. Mr. Fox

   B. King Bear

4. Who had a tail that got in his way?

   A. Mr. Fox

   B. King Bear

5. Who spoke with Mother Nature?

   A. Mr. Fox

   B. King Bear

6. Who took eggs from the henhouse?

   A. Mr. Fox

   B. King Bear

Name _____

7. Look back at both stories. Complete the graphic organizer.

Title	Title
Event 1	Event 1
Event 2	Event 2
Event 3	Event 3
Conclusion	Conclusion

8. Look back at both stories. Which one did you enjoy more? Explain your answer.

_____

_____

_____

_____

_____

Snow Day!

Ben turned off the alarm clock, jumped up, and ran to the window. Everything was covered with snow! He ran downstairs where his mother was making pancakes.

"Good morning," his mother said. "School is canceled."

"Hooray!" Ben yelled as he quickly ate his breakfast.

After breakfast, Ben got dressed and ran outside. His best friend, Mia, was already rolling a big snowball. Ben started to help, and the two made three large snowballs. Soon, the friends had a tall snowman.

They moved over to Mia's yard and began digging a hole in a deep snowdrift. Then, they reinforced the sides with small snowballs. They worked for a while. Finally, Mia sat back on her heels.

"Wow! That's a cool fort!" Mia said.

"Yeah!" Ben said. He was breathless and happy.

Then, his mother came to the door and called Ben. She handed him a picnic lunch. The friends sat in the fort and munched away. Ben knew that Mia agreed with him when he said, "Snow days are my favorite!"

The Snowy Day

"Wake up, wake up!" Kevin called, as he jumped on Keisha's bed. "Look at the snow! School is canceled."

Keisha was wide awake when she heard her twin's announcement. "Hooray!" She jumped out of bed and ran to the window.

After breakfast, the twins cleaned the kitchen. Then, they quickly gathered ingredients. Mom helped them with the oven, and they made dozens of cookies.

While the cookies were cooling, the twins made some frosting. They added colored dye. Then, they carefully decorated their cookies. Jan stood back to admire the colorful snowmen, mittens, and winter hats that lined the kitchen counters.

"What do you think?" Keisha asked. Kevin could not answer her because his mouth was full of a snowman cookie!

After lunch, the twins played board games in front of the fireplace. Mom made hot chocolate. Then, they drank their hot chocolate while they watched a movie.

Keisha smiled happily. She said, "Snow days are my favorite!"

Name _____

Number each set of events in the order they happened.

1. "Snow Day!"

_____ Ben and Mia built a fort.

_____ Ben ate breakfast.

_____ Ben and Mia built a snowman.

2. "The Snowy Day"

_____ Kevin and Keisha frosted cookies.

_____ Kevin and Keisha baked dozens of cookies.

_____ Kevin and Keisha drank hot chocolate.

Write the character's name who said each quote.

3. _____ "Wow! That's a cool fort!"

4. _____ "Look at the snow!"

5. _____ "What do you think?"

6. Look back at both stories. Which way would you rather spend your snow day? Explain your answer.

_____

_____

_____

_____

Name _____

7. Look back at both passages. Complete the graphic organizer.

Snow Day!	The Snowy Day
Characters:	Characters:
Setting:	Setting:
Event 1:	Event 1:
Event 2:	Event 2:
Event 3:	Event 3:

8. Write two or three sentences to explain how the two stories are alike.

_____

_____

_____

_____

Family Project

"But, Dad," Denise said, "My favorite show is on. I don't want to be up here."

"Denise," Dad said, "cleaning the attic is a family project. We are all part of this family."

Denise grumbled, "Where do I have to start?"

Dad pointed at some boxes, and Denise opened one. It was full of old quilts. Denise sighed. *Why would anyone keep these?* Denise thought to herself. Then, Dad reached over her head and picked up a pink quilt. "Look! Granny made this quilt when you were born. She was so thrilled to have a granddaughter! She cried when she wrapped you in it."

Denise did not remember Granny very well. She did remember that Granny's house smelled like pumpkin pie and that Granny hugged her tightly. She loved her memories of Granny. They made her happy and sad at the same time. She wrapped the quilt around her shoulders.

"Are all of the boxes full of memories, Dad?" Denise asked.

"Yes," Dad said. "This attic is filled with family memories."

"Well, then," said Denise, "Let's get to work."

On the Farm

"What's wrong, Jacob?" Grandpa asked.

"Grandpa, I love you, and I love staying at the farm. But, I don't love all the chores we do here," Jacob said. "It's summer, and I want to go fishing, not work all day."

"I see," Grandpa said. "Well, Jacob, this is a family farm. Everybody works together. Do you like the eggs Granny cooks for breakfast?"

Jacob nodded.

"Of course you do," Grandpa said. "Do you like drinking milk?"

"Yes," Jacob said.

"The milk comes from the cows we are milking right now, right?" Grandpa said. "We don't buy our milk at the store like your mom does."

"I guess I knew that," Jacob said thoughtfully.

"Did you know that your dad and Uncle Cole built the dock you stand on at the pond?" Grandpa asked. "Everybody works together."

"I see," Jacob said.

"OK, Jacob, please take the eggs in, and then we can go fishing," Grandpa said.

"I can't right now," Jacob said. "I asked Granny to bake a pie, so I need to go pick some blueberries!"

Name _____

Answer each question.

1. Which character is cleaning the attic?

   A. Denise

   B. Jacob

   C. both

2. Which character is working with a grandparent?

   A. Denise

   B. Jacob

   C. both

3. Which character wants to watch TV?

   A. Denise

   B. Jacob

   C. both

4. Which character learned a lesson?

   A. Denise

   B. Jacob

   C. both

5. How do you think Denise feels when Dad tells her about the quilt? Explain your answer.

   _____

   _____

6. How do you think Jacob feels when Grandpa tells him about the dock? Explain your answer.

   _____

   _____

Name _____

7. Look back at both passages. Complete the graphic organizer.

Family Project	**On the Farm**
Main character _____ How the main character feels at the beginning of the story:	Main character _____ How the main character feels at the beginning of the story:
Two things that happen to the character during the story:	Two things that happen to the character during the story:
How the character feels during the story:	How the character feels during the story:

8. Look back at both stories. Write a summary of the lessons Denise and Jacob learned.

_____

_____

_____

_____

The Two Melons
(A Chinese Tale, adapted)

An old woman sat in her garden. A bird with a broken wing fell to the ground in front of her. The woman took the bird home and gently nursed him back to health. Then, she released him.

Later, the bird flew back and dropped a seed. The old woman planted the seed.

The woman was very poor. She hoped the seed would produce something to eat. When a large melon grew, she happily cut into it. She was surprised when gold and silver coins poured out of the melon! She paid her bills and lived happily ever after.

The woman's cruel sister had watched these events. She threw rocks at birds until she hurt one. She nursed it back to health and released it.

The bird flew back and gave the cruel woman a seed. She planted it and then she spent a lot of money that she did not have. When the melon grew, she eagerly cut into it. She was shocked when ashes and sawdust poured out of it.

The Enchanted Waterfall
(A Japanese Tale, adapted)

A good son worked hard to take care of his parents. His mother was a happy woman. But, his father was ungrateful. He complained all day. He did not like the food. He did not like their house. He wanted more all of the time.

One day, the son was working in the forest. He stopped when he discovered a new waterfall. He placed a gourd under the falls to catch some clear water.

When he lifted the gourd to drink, it was filled with jewels! The son rushed home to his parents. His father happily spent the money and sent his son back to the waterfall every day for more.

The father bragged to his friends about the waterfall. Soon, the friends schemed to follow the son.

After the son left, the men argued with each other. Each wanted to be the first to fill his gourd. The loudest man won and placed his gourd under the falls. When he lifted the gourd, it was filled only with water.

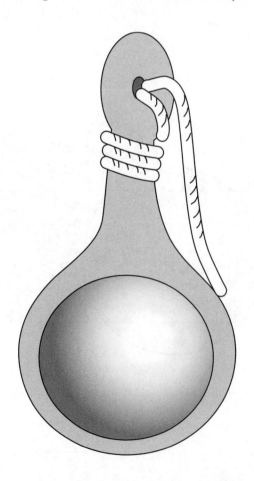

Name _____

Circle the correct answer.

1. Why does the old woman care for the bird with the broken wing?

   A. She wants a magic seed.   **B.** She is poor.

   C. She is kind and caring.   **D.** The bird is pretty.

2. Why does the bird give the magic seed to the old woman?

   A. She is poor.   **B.** The bird wants to thank her.

   C. The bird drops it.   **D.** The bird is careless.

3. Why does the cruel sister throw rocks at birds?

   A. She wants a magic seed.   **B.** She is poor.

   C. She is kind and caring.   **D.** She hates birds.

4. Why did the son find jewels in his gourd?

   A. He was thirsty.

   B. He was good and hardworking.

   C. He was greedy and wanted to be first.

   D. Jewels are often found in gourds.

5. Why do the men follow the good son?

   A. The father tells them to.

   B. They are thirsty.

   C. They want to find where he is getting the treasure.

   D. They are lost.

6. Why did the man find water in his gourd?

   A. He was thirsty.

   B. He was good and hardworking.

   C. He was greedy and wanted to be first.

   D. The gourd was magical.

Name _____

7. Look back at both passages. Complete the graphic organizer.

The Old Woman	**The Good Son**
Character traits:	Character traits:
What she does:	What he does:
What happens:	What happens:

8. Look back at both stories. Write a summary of the lesson the two main characters learned.

_____

_____

_____

_____

_____

Fiction

The Pine Tree

Pine Tree stood in the forest. "I do not like my needles," he said. "Other trees have beautiful leaves. I wish that I had golden leaves." A fairy granted his wish. The tree was happy with his shiny new leaves.

That day, a man came. "What beautiful leaves you have!" he said. He picked the tree's leaves and put them into a bag. The tree cried.

"I do not want golden leaves," he said. "I want leaves made of glass." The fairy granted his wish, and the tree was happy!

That day, the wind blew through the forest, and the leaves fell from the tree. They lay cracked and broken on the ground, and the tree cried.

"I do not want leaves made of glass," he said. "I want green leaves because they are best." Once again, the fairy granted his wish, and the tree was happy.

That day, a goat ate the tree's leaves, and the tree cried.

"I do not want green leaves," he said. "I want green needles." The fairy granted his wish. The tree was finally happy!

The Ugly Duckling

by Hans Christian Andersen (adapted)

A mother duck had four ducklings. Three were cute ducklings. One was an ugly duckling. All of her ducklings were good and kind, and she loved them dearly.

She took the ducklings to the pond at the park. Another duck bit the ugly duckling's tail. Soon, many ducks were biting the ugly duckling. Mother Duck cried, "Stop! Why are you hurting my duckling?"

"He is so ugly!" they said.

"My duckling has not hurt you," Mother Duck said.

Mother Duck took her ducklings to the farm pond. The cow laughed at the ugly duckling. Soon, all of the farm animals were laughing too. They said, "Look at that ugly duckling!"

The ugly duckling waddled into the bushes. He cried. He lived alone for many months. Then, he came back to the pond for a good swim. At the edge of the pond, he looked into the water. He did not see an ugly duckling! He saw a beautiful swan gazing back at him! It was a happy day for the ugly duckling.

Name _____

Answer each question.

1. How do you think Pine Tree feels when he says, "I wish that I had golden leaves"? Explain your answer.

_____

_____

_____

2. How do you think Pine Tree feels when he sees his new glass leaves? Explain your answer.

_____

_____

_____

3. How do you think the ugly duckling feels when Mother Duck says, "Stop! Why are you hurting my duckling?" Explain your answer.

_____

_____

_____

4. How do you think the ugly duckling feels when the farm animals laugh at him? Explain your answer.

_____

_____

_____

Name _____

5. Look back at both passages. Complete the graphic organizer.

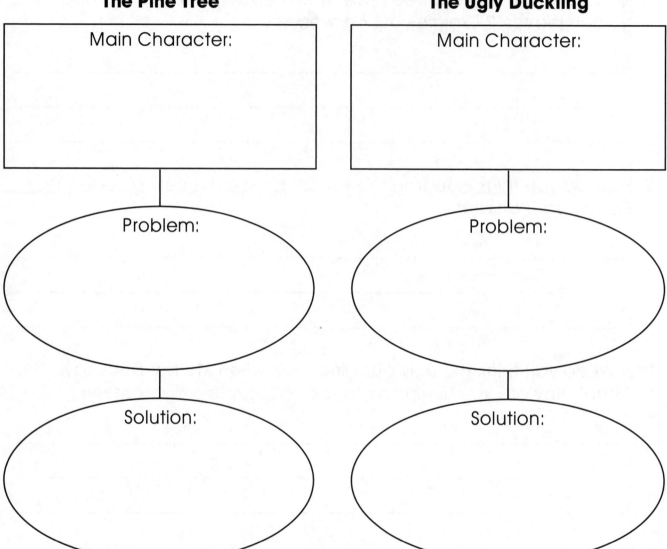

The Pine Tree

Main Character:

Problem:

Solution:

The Ugly Duckling

Main Character:

Problem:

Solution:

6. Think about how the main character of each story feels at the beginning and the end of the story. Tell how Pine Tree and the ugly duckling are alike or different.

_____

_____

_____

_____

Answer Key

Pages 7–8
1. false; 2. true; 3. true; 4. false; 5. B; 6. A; 7. C; 8. Answers will vary but may include: The mother owl sits on the eggs until they hatch. The parents teach the babies to care for themselves after they hatch. A baby owl is soft and white and covered with down. 9. Answers will vary.

Pages 11–12
1. A; 2. B; 3. C; 4. Answers will vary but may include some insects produce a spray. Some insects are colorful. Insects can cause pain. 5. Answers will vary but may include: "My Colorful Friend" is a poem, has a speaker who is telling the poem, talks about bugs the character draws; Both passages are about bugs and feature real ladybugs; "Guarding a Bug's Life" gives information about real bugs, tells how bugs protect themselves, tells about reasons that bugs need protection. 6. Answers will vary.

Pages 15–16
1. B; 2. B; 3. A; 4. A; 5. false; 6. true; 7. Answers will vary but may include: (*Boom!*): Stay away from water during a storm. Stay in a sturdy building or a car with closed windows. Stay away from metal. (*Raining and Pouring*): Storms are more likely to happen in spring or summer. Storms are more likely to happen later in the day. Lightning is an electric current. 8. Answers will vary.

Pages 19–20
1. needs; 2. shelter; 3. want; 4. both; 5. Answers will vary but may include the idea that the shoes are a need because Rachel needs them for soccer practice. 6. Answers will vary but may include the idea that the game is a want because Rachel wants to play with it. 7. Answers will vary but may include: (*Needs*) shelter: People need shelter to protect them from heat, rain, and cold. water: People need water to drink, to bathe in, and to cook with. food: People need food to eat so they will have energy.(*Wants*) books: People want books because they enjoy reading them. TVs: People want TVs to watch their favorite shows. games: People want games because they enjoy playing them. 8. Answers will vary.

Pages 23–24
1. Answers will vary but may include the idea that the country mouse means that they will have to wait for the crops to grow before they can eat. 2. Answers will vary but may include the idea that it is better to have a little bit of food and live in peace than to have a lot of food and live in fear. 3. Answers will vary but should include details about students' home areas that support their answers. 4. Answers will vary. 5. Answers will vary but may include: (*Country*) bare fields, farms, farmers, tractors, wagons; (*Both*) cars, stores, offices, people; (*Town/City*) a busy place, buses, trains, apartments; 6. Answers will vary but may include that people live in houses, drive cars, work, and play in both places. 7. Answers will vary but may include that people can ride trains in the city and people can ride tractors in the country.

Pages 27–28
1. C; 2. A; 3 Answers will vary but may include the idea that the prince is sad because the text says that he sadly returned home. 4. Answers will vary but may include the idea that the prince is happy because he wanted to marry and he has found a real princess. The text says that they lived happily ever after. 5. Answers will vary but may include: Prince, hero, and father. 6. Answers will vary but may include: (*The Princess and the Pea*) is a fairy tale and a princess is tested by a queen. Both passages involve royalty and a prince gets married; (*Real Royalty*) is about a real prince who is a father, a hero, and a helicopter pilot. 7. Answers will vary.

Pages 31–32
1. C; 2. C; 3. Answers will vary. 4. Answers will vary. 5. true; 6. false; 7. Answers will vary but may include: (*Cool in the Pool*): Stay cool in the pool. Both: You can have fun in water. (*Swimming Safety*): Stay away from drains. Keep a phone near the pool. Know how to swim. 8. Answers will vary but should include one important swimming safety rule, such as learning to swim. Students should include logical reasons to support their opinions.

Pages 35–36
1. helmet; 2. adult; 3. bright; 4. B; 5. A; 6. B; 7. The main idea will vary but should include the idea that it is important to be safe when you ride your bicycle. Supporting details will vary but may include to choose a bike that is the right height for you. Bring a helmet that fits you correctly. Stop and check both ways for cars. 8. Answers will vary.

Answer Key

Pages 39–40

1. Independence Day;
2. flags; 3. Sparklers; 4. aerial;
5. Answers will vary but may include: People have parades. People may hang flags on their homes. People may have cookouts or picnics. 6. The passage was written to inform the reader about the Fourth of July. Students should use details from the passage to explain their answers. 7. The passage was written to inform the reader about fireworks. Students should use details from the passage to explain their answers. 8. Answers will vary but may include: (*Firecrackers*) one kind of fireworks; loud bang; are rolled into a tube; have flash powder inside; (*Sparklers*) one kind of fireworks; burn slowly; are made on a metal wire; the wire gets very hot; (*Fireworks*) seen in the sky at night; have a shell that is launched from a mortar; have mixed powders; may be many colors;
9. Answers will vary.

Pages 43–44

1. animal; 2. medicine;
3. communicate; 4. vet;
5. bathe; 6. true; 7. true;
8. false; 9. Answers will vary but may include: (*Dogs*) You must play with your dog and give her exercise. You should bathe a dog. Dogs bark, growl, and whine. (*Both*) Take your pet to the vet once a year. You should give medicine to your pet. Caring for your pet is a big responsibility. (*Cats*) Cats were first tamed in Egypt. Cats bathe themselves. Cats meow and purr. 10. Answers will vary.

Pages 47–48

1. C; 2. A; 3. C; 4. B; 5. (*Frog*) First stage: egg, The frog lays an egg in the water. Second stage: tadpole, The tadpole hatches and swims in the water. Third stage: froglet, The tadpole sprouts back legs and becomes a froglet. Fourth stage: frog, The froglet's tail completely disappears, and all four legs form. (*Butterfly*) First stage: egg, The butterfly lays its egg on a leaf or a stem. Second stage: larva, The larva, or caterpillar, hatches from the egg and begins to eat leaves and grass. Third stage: pupa, The larva forms a chrysalis or a cocoon. Fourth stage: butterfly, The butterfly breaks out of its cocoon. 6. Answers will vary. 7. Answers will vary.

Pages 51–52

1. Kyle received a toy vacuum cleaner as a gift. 2. Kyle followed his mom when she turned the real vacuum cleaner on. 3. Julian's father thought Julian might be a good player. 4. His father painted court lines in the front yard. 5. B; 6. A; 7. Answers will vary but may include: (*Kyle*) collects vacuum cleaners, vacuumed the classroom and the principal's office, is paid to fix vacuum cleaners; (*Both*) started very young and had a lot of family support; (*Julian*) loves basketball, both parents played basketball, played basketball at school. 8. Answers will vary.

Pages 55–56

1. true; 2. false; 3. false; 4. true;
5. false; 6. seed; 7. bury;
8. stem; 9. Answers will vary but may include that seeds may travel in wind or water. Some seeds are built to fly or float, and they are very lightweight. Seeds may travel when animals eat them. If the seeds are not digested, they may be dropped in some other place. They may grow where they are dropped. 10. Answers will vary but may include: (*How Seeds Travel*) Farmers plant some seeds. Seeds may stick to some animals' fur. Animals may bury some seeds. (*Both*)All plants start as seeds. (*How Plants Grow*) First, a seed is planted. The seed cracks, and a stem and roots break out of the seed. The stem continues to grow, and leaves and flowers appear. 11. Answers will vary, but may include that both authors wrote the passages to give the reader true information about plants. The author of *How Seeds Travel* gives information about the way seeds are moved around. The author of *How Plants Grow* gives information about what happens to a seed after it is planted.

Pages 59–60

1. Answers will vary but may include the president of the United States has many jobs.
2. Answers will vary but may include: A. The president is in charge of all soldiers and of telling them where to go. B. He makes deals with other countries called treaties. C. He helps make new laws.
3. Answers will vary but may include that America has many symbols. 4. Answers will vary but may include: A. The flag is a symbol that is also called "Old Glory." B. The bald eagle stands for strength, courage, and freedom. C. The Statue of Liberty is a symbol of freedom.
5. Answers will vary but may include: (*Symbol*) president of the United States; (*Facts about symbol*) He makes many speeches. He may give awards to special people. (*Symbol*)

94

Answer Key

American flag; (*Facts about symbol*) has 50 stars, one for each state and has 13 stripes, one for each original colony; (*Symbol*) bald eagle; (*Facts about symbol*) US national bird; stands for courage, strength, and freedom; (*Symbol*) Statue of Liberty;(*Facts about symbol*) stands for freedom, was a gift from France, has 354 stairs; 6. Answers will vary.

Pages 63–64
1. D; 2. C; 3. C; 4. D; 5. Answers will vary but may include: (*Desert*) Words to know: humid, extreme, nocturnal, adapted; Facts I learned: Deserts are very dry. Desert animals can live on very little water. Many plants grow in the desert. Questions I still have: Answers will vary. (*Wetlands*) Words to know: freshwater, spongy, adaptations, features; Facts I learned: Wetlands are all over the world. Some wetlands change throughout the year. Marshes, bogs, and swamps are all wetlands. Questions I still have: Answers will vary. 6. Answers will vary.

Pages 67–68
1. the mountains; Supporting reasons will vary but may include that the characters are near a stream. Erin is planning to go hiking on a steep trail. They are planning to go fishing in a lake. 2. the beach; Supporting reasons will vary but may include that the brothers are splashing in the waves. They kicked through the sand. They plan to collect seashells the next day. 3. Rashad; Supporting reasons will vary but may include that he helps Zach hang his swimsuit and towel on the clothesline.

4. Answers will vary but may include (*Family Vacation*) Beginning: Erin is eating hot dogs around the campfire with her family. Middle: Erin looks at the stars and plans what she will do the next day. End: The family goes to sleep in their tent. (*Summer Vacation*) Beginning: The boys are playing in the waves. Middle: The boys eat hot dogs around a campfire with their family. End: The boys go to sleep in their sleeping bags. 5. Answers will vary but may include that both stories are about families that are on vacation. Both families have hot dogs for dinner. Both families are going fishing. 6. Answers will vary but may include that one family has two girls, and the other family has two boys. One family is at the beach, and the other is at the mountains.

Pages 71–72
1. A; 2. D; 3. B; 4. C; 5. B; 6. C; 7. Answers will vary but may include: (*The Hat*) Main Character: The speaker; Problem: He has a bad haircut and wants to wear his hat in school. His teacher wants him to take it off. Solution: His teacher sees his haircut and, because she is kind, tells the rest of the class that it is class hat day. (*Rapunzel*) Main Character: Rapunzel; Problem: She is trapped in a tower. Solution: A prince calls her, and she lets her hair down. They meet, fall in love, and live happily ever after. 8. Answers will vary but may include that the main characters are alike because they each have a problem with their hair. The main characters are different because one is a young child in

school and the other is a grown woman trapped in a tower.

Pages 75–76
1. Answers will vary. 2. Answers will vary. 3. A; 4. B; 5. B; 6. A; 7. Answers will vary but may include: Title: "Why Fox Wears Red;" Event 1: Fox has a dull brown coat. He sneaks around and listens to his neighbors talk. Event 2: Fox steals from his neighbors. Event 3: Mother Nature comes to catch the criminal and she sees red clay on fox's tail. Conclusion: Mother Nature turns him bright red. Title: "Why Bear Has a Stubby Tail;" Event 1: Bear is a happy king of the forest. He is only worried about food. Event 2: He hears animals talking about him and the fact that he has no tail. Event 3: He begs Mother Nature to give him a tail. Conclusion: The tail gets in his way, and he begs Mother Nature to take it away. 8. Answers will vary.

Pages 79–80
1. 3, 1, 2; 2. 2, 1, 3; 3. Mia; 4. Kevin; 5. Keisha; 6. Answers will vary. 7. Answers will vary but may include: (*Snow Day!*) Characters: Ben, Mother, and Mia. Setting: Outside, on a snowy day. Event 1: School is canceled. Event 2: Ben and Mia build a snowman. Event 3: Ben and Mia build a snow fort. (*A Snowy Day*) Characters: Kevin, Keisha, and Mom. Setting: Indoors, on a snowy day. Event 1: School is canceled. Event 2: Kevin and Keisha bake cookies. Event 3: Kevin and Keisha play a board game. 8. Answers will vary but may include that the stories are alike because both stories happen on a day when school is canceled because of snow.

Answer Key

Pages 83–84

I. A; 2. B; 3. A; 4. C; 5. Answers will vary but may include the idea that Denise did not realize that she would learn about her family as she helped to clean up the attic. 6. Answers will vary but may include the idea that Jacob did not realize how much work goes into the farm. 7. Answers will vary but may include: (*Family Project*) Main character: Denise; How the character feels at the beginning of the story: Denise wants to watch TV instead of help her family clean the attic. Two things that happen to the character during the story: Denise finds a box full of quilts that she does not think anyone should keep. Denise finds out that her Granny made one of the quilts for her. How the character feels during the story: Denise remembers her Granny and the things she loved about her. She wants to know what is in the other boxes. (*On the Farm*) Main character: Jacob; How the character feels at the beginning of the story: He wants to go fishing instead of helping his grandfather with the chores. Two things that happen to the character during the story: His grandfather points out that the milk and eggs he likes come from the work on the farm. His grandfather also tells him that his father and uncle built the dock he stands on when he is fishing. How the character feels during the story: Jacob begins to realize that the work on the farm produces things for the family, things that he enjoys. 8. Answers will vary but may include the idea that each child learned that families work together to achieve something important.

Pages 87–88

I. C; 2. B; 3. A; 4. B; 5. C; 6. C; 7. Answers will vary but may include: (*The Old Woman*) Main character: the old woman; Character Traits: gentle, caring; What she does: She finds a bird with a broken wing, nurses it back to health, and releases it. What happens: The bird brings a seed to the woman. She plants it and grows a melon. She opens the melon and finds silver. (*The Good Son*) Main character: the son; Character Traits: hardworking, selfless; What he does: He puts a gourd under a waterfall to catch a drink of water. What happens: When he looks, the gourd is filled with jewels. He takes the jewels back to his parents. 8. Answers will vary but may include the idea that each character learns that it pays to be of good character.

Pages 91–92

I. Answers will vary but may include the idea that he feels ugly, and he wants to have leaves that are prettier than the leaves the other trees have. 2. Answers will vary but may include the idea that he feels proud of his shiny new leaves. 3. Answers will vary but may include the idea that she feels hurt and confused because they are hurting her duckling because of the way he looks. 4. Answers will vary but may include the idea that his feelings are hurt. 5. Answers will vary but may include: (*The Pine Tree*) Main Character: The Pine Tree; Problem: He thinks that his needles are ugly. Solution: He asks a fairy to change his needles, but each change does not work out. Finally, he decides that green needles are best after all. (*The Ugly Duckling*) Main Character: The Ugly Duckling; Problem: All of the other animals think he is very ugly. Solution: He grows into a beautiful swan.
6. Answers will vary but may include the idea that Pine Tree judges himself by his looks, while others judge the ugly duckling because of his looks. Both stories are about the way the characters look.